Beauty in Love and Sorrows

Beauty in Love and Sorrows

sheila atienza

Privilege Digital Media

Beauty in Love and Sorrows
Copyright © 2021 by Sheila Atienza

Published by
Privilege Digital Media
Richmond
British Columbia, Canada

All rights reserved.

No part of this book may be reproduced in any manner whatsoever without written permission except in the case of brief quotations embodied in critical articles and reviews.

This book is a work of fiction. The names, characters, places, and incidents in the story either are the product of the author's imagination or are used fictitiously. Any similarities to any person or persons, places, and events are purely coincidental.

Paperback ISBN-13 :
978-1-990408-03-8

E-book ISBN:
978-1-990408-04-5

Subjects:

FAMILY & RELATIONSHIPS / Love & Romance
POETRY / Subjects & Themes / Death, Grief, Loss
FAMILY & RELATIONSHIPS / Divorce & Separation

Thema Subjects:

Narrative theme: Love and relationships
Fiction: narrative themes
Adult & contemporary romance

CONTENTS

A Quick Look: Select Excerpts   xi
Dedication   xv

One
Romancing

1 Colours   3

2 Mythical   5

3 Melodious   8

4 To Honour   10

5 Take Delight   11

6 Enamoured   12

Two
Holding On

7 Wondering   17

8 Next Time   18

9 Hole   19

10 Domain Of Love   21

Three
Devotion

11	Rare	25
12	More Of	27
13	Eagerness To Forever	29
14	Convince	31
15	Uneventful	33
16	Genuine	35
17	Cherish	37

Four
Hope And Affirmation

18	Worthy	41
19	Unfolding	43
20	Creative Self	44
21	Focus	45
22	Someone To Care	46
23	Closer To The Soul	48
24	What Might We Gain	49
25	A Chance To Grow	50
26	Infinite	51
27	In Time	52
28	Good Stuff	54

Five
Missing Part

29	Jive	59
30	Whisper With Enchantment	61
31	Lost In The Dark	63
32	Promise Of The Recent Past	64
33	Kiss Of Nothingness	66
34	For The Sake Of Sanity	68

Six
Cling

35	Some Goodness	73
36	Powerful Even To A Fool	75
37	Murmur	77
38	Rare Stone	79
39	Deepest	81
40	If Only	83

Seven
Switch Gently

41	Why	87
42	Still	89
43	I Let You	91
44	Bright And Calm	93
45	Moments That Matter	95

Eight
Perplexity

46	The What	99
47	The Game I Can't Play	101
48	Any Further	103
49	Coming Into You	105
50	Just Like That	107

Nine
Shattered

51	Instance	113
52	Predicament	115
53	To Illuminate	116
54	Precious Waking Hours	118
55	Wind Up	120
56	Villain	123
57	Regain	125

Ten
Wound And Pinch

58	Must I	129
59	Brokenness	131
60	Face The Night	133
61	Gone Wrong	135
62	Gloomy In The Mirror	137

63	Her Own Nightmare	139
64	Interior	141
65	Silver-tinted Frame	143
66	Pinch	145
67	Enough	147
68	Numbness	149
69	Can't Help	151
70	Maybe Then	153
71	Cool And Meditative	155

Eleven
Seesaw And Crack

72	Storm	159
73	What If	160
74	Shield	162
75	Very Sharp	164
76	Random	166
77	Be Over	168
78	Better Version	170
79	New Perspective	172
80	Awesome People	174

Twelve
Sundown To Sunup

81	New Glow	179
82	To Feel Again	181
83	Just Wish	184
84	Part	186
85	Indescribably Wonderful	188

About The Author   193

A QUICK LOOK: SELECT EXCERPTS

"you are a rare stone
that i would keep with me with care
and guard securely
from dusk till dawn"
- *rare stone*

"the truth is
i am almost without hope
but then my arduous faith takes me
to a point where
love could be most powerful
even to a fool"
- *powerful even to a fool*

"after the rain, the exterior dries up again
it is a welcoming occurrence
it is nature's way of manifesting
life"
- *new glow*

"i could see an image or
silhouette
some trace
of a striking human
someone
approaches through the door"
- *some goodness*

"i kept my hopes up
i kept my vibe up
the time has come
to get my feet moving
to feel the jive and
to turn my fears away"
- *jive*

"should i succumb to a kiss of nothingness
should i witness
another break of dawn
another night of hope"
- *kiss of nothingness*

"the silver-tinted little frame
that displays on the corner table
holds a landscape image
with it, comes a sweet message"
- *silver-tinted frame*

"why bother
about our carelessness
we were
simply being ourselves
enjoying the moment..."
-*moments that matter*

* * *

dedication

to you
and those who
believe in the spirit
of love
some may struggle, some may find joys
but in the end
the experience is all worth it

one

romancing

1

colours

how do i put meaning into my life
where do i look
what should i feel
is it colourful, after all
with all the shades and highlights
intensity and contrast

how do i bring meaning into your life
where do i start
what do i say
would you find it delightful, after all
with all the taste of sweetness and more
what with all the flavours, we could taste one or
we could taste all

colours
why don't i see
you're there
yet, hiding somewhere

oh, colours
will you come
into my world
paint my life
let me tap into your
features
brightness
mood, texture

let me share
beauty and radiance
with you, let me find strength
and let me enter into the world of romance

* * *

2

mythical

i am *Beauty*
i go by that name
my other
half is the one
whom i call my *Tiger*
together
we build a life
that we describe
oh, so dazzling and mightier

nothing can go wrong
so we say
in love, we savour
we explore goodness, fragrance and all

each day
seems to harmonize
well, even with
the simple promise
of eternity, as we wrap our hands in bliss
to the chain of love, we hold the keys

beyond belief
so to say
the smiles that we give
to one another
are just enough

is this happening for real
i can't help but ask
my heart has just
one answer to this
whatever this may be
till the end
of time, let it remain
the spirit of love
let it forever manifest

it can appear mythical
call it even unreal
but what is the best of it all
we build a kingdom of our own
for the first time, i feel
i am the queen of the ball

my *Tiger* says
he adores me
the warmth
that we share is
what keeps us
at night, safe and
in peace

* * *

3

melodious

my *Tiger* and i converse
in such a way that is
melodious
just like a song
that tells you
how can you make life
marvelous
and strong

Tiger is oh-so delightful
he is warm-hearted
to others, even amiable
he may not be that expressive
yet he makes me feel
i am the one
with whom he would
always
spend
his life and days
to utter the lyrics
that echo with melodies
as they rhyme

* * *

4

to honour

so wondrous, so joyful, every second
now, we are on
to celebrate
a feast
that should honour the time
the place
and the moment
the experiences
that embody
how well we have been
and how far else
we could be

* * *

5

take delight

take delight in those moments
let the stars align
and brighten up
the nights
and may our joys surround
our days
and throughout our life

* * *

6

enamoured

i watch the hours
they should go by so fast
yet
it feels as though
the hands of the clock
have not ever ticked

i sit back and relax
as you would always ask
i would do it
so gladly
for i know that
would make you candid
and jolly

i am continually enamoured
by your smiles
and by your
bright, adorable eyes
that flicker
oh, my *Tiger,* come home now

i can't wait
to hear the sound of the bell
and that tells me
you are at home, finally

* * *

two

holding on

7

wondering

sometimes, i can't help
in the middle of your absence
i start to wonder
whether
you are doing all right

what could go in your way
would you get back
intact
with your arms and hands that
could hold me tight

* * *

8

next time

would you get back
and say
"*Beauty, I*'ve missed you
so much
don't you worry
next time
I will be with you and
forever stay."

* * *

9

hole

won't we ever
get to a point
or even wake up one day
and realize
this is not what it should be
that we overlook
where we are

did we even see
if there's a hole
that needs patching up
or what if
we lose track
of the journey
or the path
that we ought to take

* * *

10

domain of love

what would happen
to the whole domain of love
that
we have built

are we ever going
to keep
holding on and
seeing through it

may our fears
not persist
nor envelope our being
may such formidable, frightening
thoughts disappear

let me clear my mind and
end my pondering
and let our shining memories
linger

***

three

devotion

11

rare

"Beauty," i could hear *Tiger* calling me
on the night, i found myself
as i awoke from my madness
he tells me to keep up
to keep hoping with such
an unquestioning heart

what would i do
what should i feel
is this rare? is this real
my heart reflects
my endless
fascination
with love
my ever deep affection
my ever devotion to our little world
we gently build and call home

* * *

12

more of

my story would not ever
ever go on
nor it would even begin
without him, my *Tiger*
i wonder
how would i
spend
my days

i know he is
worthy of my utmost care
with whom i wish i could explore
more of
my daily, joyous hours

* * *

13

eagerness to forever

i hope he could hear me
i feel as if he is just there
the mere thoughts of him help me
wrap up my day

he inspires me to become what i could be
with eagerness
i shall welcome my day

i wish and
i look forward to another
brightening moment
when i could be
with him again

what a great feeling to wake up
to feel the love
to feel the warmth
to feel and hope
our moments could find the path
to reaching our forever

* * *

14

convince

i believe in us, together
i know we can be
i can follow
i can grow

let us take our time
just like what you would
always say

many days have passed and
i always try
to think of your presence, to remember

i would convince myself and say
it doesn't matter
if you're with me or not

i feel
after all, love is real
for you and me, my *Tiger*

* * *

15

uneventful

i refused to notice
without you
i would have to face
another long, uneventful day

i know it does not please
but should that be enough
to cause
one to panic

in spirit
i know you are
in here, in my heart
and that should be enough

* * *

16

genuine

others could say
that i'm silly
they could say whatever
they want to say

truth, i could tell
i've always been
genuine and
loyal

if i would have to say it
to you, my dear
to my soul
to my heart
i would not hesitate
and i shall always say it

* * *

17

cherish

the marvel in the air, every moment i feel
about you
about me, about us

to you
my *Tiger*
my heart, i entrust

if this is not going to last
let tomorrow
decide, my dear
i am happy now
and that's what matters

i treasure this feeling
i love, love this thing
i have faith that you would be here
no matter
how long you may have been
away
from me, oh dear

that is the wondrous thing
about you, and
in what i feel
about love, and even in
our sweet nothings
with you, i would always
choose to live

* * *

four

hope and affirmation

18

worthy

today, i affirm
to *God,* the highest power
i am, and
i will always be
a believer

despite my
weaknesses
with *God's* grace
i am still
a worthy being

i welcome and
embrace
God's love and the life
that *He* had bestowed
upon my whole being

* * *

19

unfolding

i am relaxed and
i am feeling great - trusting
in a higher plan
that is unfolding

i enjoy what i do
i am grateful for having been given
the chance to begin
another day with excitement

* * *

20

creative self

i allow
my creative self
to explore the universe
as it allows me
to enjoy
such adventure

* * *

21

focus

i just focus on this
moment
i am privileged to do this
with such a gift
to see life in its finest

* * *

22

someone to care

i could see at the top
of the mountain
i could rejoice
there is hope
i could cheer and sing

with the top of my voice
i have someone
to care
my *Tiger* is the one
for which my life i share

* * *

23

closer to the soul

i appreciate
all the experiences
i could get
from doing this

i, for one, could attest
absence
could make one's heart
grow with love
even closer
to the soul

* * *

24

what might we gain

despite a possibility
that one could get hurt
in the end
who knows
what lessons might we get
what wisdom might we gain

*　*　*

25

a chance to grow

i look at this as fate
would have it
a chance to grow
so i could show off my confidence

i accept that the higher universe
knows
what's best
for you and me
and perfectly gives us chances

* * *

26

infinite

i am in a place
of infinite possibility
everyone has a place
in this universe
and *God* is leading me
towards the path
He wants me
to be

* * *

27

in time

i will eventually reach
my desires and plans
and it will happen
in time

i'll have to keep going
i shall enjoy
every little thing
i receive today, tomorrow, and beyond

everything that happens
is in accordance
to *God's* will and
His masterplan

He is my protector
with *Him,* i entrust my future
he will take me to a place
and into a moment beyond compare

* * *

28

good stuff

for now, i shall dwell
to keep
my whole being
alive and well

i just have to keep doing, putting
good stuff out there
and working on my craft
good things will come my way

yes, that is how
it is going to be
that is
what it should be

i can't wait to experience
a life full of marvel
even if it must begin
past today

* * *

five

missing part

29

jive

i kept my hopes up
i kept my vibe up
the time has come
to get my feet moving
to feel the jive and
to turn my fears away

finally
the time
has come
to find the piece
that part in my heart
that has been missing

three, two, and
one more hour
my heart screams out
come here, my dear *Tiger*
let us embrace
once again

* * *

30

whisper with enchantment

now, where could you be
you never came
the last time i remember
we looked up the skies, held our hands
to our hearts, you said, the heaven is our witness
as you have, long before
uttered, even
whispered
with enchantment

my *Tiger*
where does this lead me
must i
listen to this heart

* * *

31

lost in the dark

i was hoping you would be here
by now
same place
same time
what could have happened
my *Tiger*

doesn't faith have power
i held onto our words
but they seem
to have gotten
lost in the dark

* * *

32

promise of the recent past

vividly, i recall
all
the sweet words
the touch of our hands
chains of romances
our blazing passions
where have all these
gone

my sweet *Tiger*
were you lost
and --
have you never
found a way
to get back

i've waited this long
and yet
i could not see
even
a glimpse
of you
and even the promise
of our recent past

* * *

33

kiss of nothingness

should i keep
waiting
til i
could see you

how many more
days of
uncertainty will i
need to endure

should i succumb to a kiss of nothingness
should i witness
another break of dawn
another night of hope

should i keep
dreaming
should i keep wanting
to win this thing

why do i have to worry
this much
i just need a word from you
how hard could that be

i am continuing
to strongly wonder
with you
do i still matter

* * *

34

for the sake of sanity

my *Tiger*, my dear
would you please
give me
some signs
some clues, perhaps

difficult it may be
but for the sake of my sanity
could you at least be here
even for just a day
even for just a fraction of time

your complete silence
could be ultra deafening
it is way above and beyond
what my mind
could comprehend

* * *

six

cling

35

some goodness

then, some good works from
heaven occurred
as though some angels from
high above
gathered
and rejoiced with hymns

i could see an image or
silhouette
some trace
of a striking human
someone
approaches through the door

if i must be dreaming
let me stay in that moment
you just don't know
how blissful
how gleeful
this has caused my heart

clearly, the message from
heaven
is unfolding
i've been longing
for such
a happy scene

i wish to enter and
be in it
just like seeing
an actor playing
a lead role in a romantic flick
or even series

* * *

36

powerful even to a fool

the truth is
i am almost without hope
but then my arduous faith takes me
to a point where
love could be most powerful
even to a fool

a reverberating sound that pulsates
through my
senses
in my heart, it thumps so loud
it tells me
to give it a go and try
then i realized
yes, this is it
that is something
for which i have been waiting
all this time, and
every moment

* * *

37

murmur

i am without words
i thought i could just give
a warm smile
and even a warm touch
could save the day

what could i expect
from now on that you are here
should i just cling onto the moment
and not be mindful of
where is this thing going

i would love to listen to your enchanting voice
your sound with a loving murmur
what is it that bothers you
my dear *Tiger*
please let me wonder
no more

* * *

38

rare stone

all of a sudden
i wrapped my arms around you
like i would never
let you go
ever
again

i tell myself
you would remain
the most precious of all
the people
i will have ever met
in my lifetime

my *Tiger*
you are a rare stone
that i would keep with me with care
and guard securely
from dusk till dawn
and
all the hours of my day

* * *

39

deepest

once again, we held our hands
i felt you
the touch that slipped through my hair
and my forehead
that
i almost perspire with anxiety
and that penetrated
through the pores of my skin

and very slowly
we took a few steps

you continued on
as you lay
your fingers on my
almost soppy face
gradually moving through the back of my neck
it tickled me a bit
down towards
the deepest of my bones
you could see how cheery and excited
that has made me

* * *

40

if only

oh, *my Tiger,* if you only knew it
if you could only witness
every part of my madness and every bit
of what i feel

if you could only see how my spirit
almost entrapped every part of me
all i could see is only
you, amid my daily
distractions and chores
if you could only be there
all the many days i had to endure

all those instances
seemed just a tiny bit
of sacrifices
they all exist
because i knew
every part between us
would fill up our senses
that would be enough for me to say
we could make it

with each other, we would get
to where we want to be
our loving spirits
will thrive
and will forever be
here
in our entire
bodies
in our hearts

* * *

seven

switch gently

41

why

it was strange to notice
the look in your eyes
the sound of your voice
and how you kept your silence

you said you were tired
i thought that must be it
i could understand that
and yes
why
wouldn't i

* * *

42

still

it was such a long journey
you might have struggled
on --
your way back

but dear, how would i ever know it
if you would not
open up to me from the start

"how was it, my *Tiger?*"
i asked gently

but you stand still and with such an expression
and just a few words
that would come out of you
i am still without a clue

* * *

43

i let you

i respect
your gestures
i would not insist
if you don't feel
the need for you to open up

your actions are enough
i let you sigh
i let you breathe
i would be glad
to see you relaxed

lay your head on the brown pillow
take some time
i let you
be
by yourself

***

44

bright and calm

tomorrow when you see the brightness of day
we can take a walk
by the seashore
listen to the chirping sounds
that seem to emanate from around
the outside world
from the tall pine trees, and
from as far as
the blue skies
just like how things used to be

here we go, my dear
i could see you are
now, somewhat calm
and hopefully comforted
by those simple scenarios
that we used to enjoy

we were strolling, laughing, and
running
we were always
catching up, with our breaths, with those
gentle, loving kisses

* * *

45

moments that matter

all we could think of doing at the time was
to allow the hours
to stand still
why bother about our carelessness
we were simply
being ourselves, enjoying the moment

and all that matters
we were next to each other
lying on the ground
what with those pristine white sands

and who could forget about
all the getaways
that we've had
a week filled with fascination
as we stroll
the wonder of *Paris*
three cool
nights in *New York*
some nights of fun and music in *Vegas*

with those
incredible experiences
we could not ever see
what could ever
be wrong

such moments that matter
we always look back and
we could bet
we could do this
lifelong

* * *

eight

perplexity

46

the what

then comes the biggest question, i asked
with my seemingly surprised, screechy
pitch
that could almost
be heard
throughout the top
of the *New York's
Empire State*

"what?"
that was mind-boggling
for the second time, i asked again
i gestured, then kept silent

a few more moments
i pretended as though nothing happened
you could see i almost refused to listen
the moment i heard
you would be gone again

you said, for just a while
really
there was sarcasm in my tone
how could you think
of even doing that
when you're just recently back

* * *

47

the game i can't play

there must be something
i thought to myself
"why don't you just tell me,
what was exactly happening?"

i can't get into this
guessing game
in which
it would seem
you would want me to play

why would i

is it fair
how much is at stake
or should i say
at such a point
you don't care

* * *

48

any further

you look afar
like you would always do
another time, another point of
silence
you would not go on
any further

you took a few more
steps away
should i keep silent or
insist further
don't i deserve to hear
the truth, my dear

* * *

49

coming into you

how unfortunate
that you could not say it
was it better off this time
without your words

why can't you profess it
will you tell me, please
why not say it straight
to my weary face

although i could not be sure
how would i take it
whatever that might be
i need to hear it

was there something
bothering you
a problem at work or
was there a new person
mysteriously
alluring
coming into you
i mean, really
coming into your life

* * *

50

just like that

you could readily decide
to take no notice of the would-be paradise
we slowly build, baby

could this be just
a made-up story
you seem so fixed
with all these

how easy was it
that in a flash
the world i've known would seem to vanish
like a spirit that detaches from the body

i asked that you stay, but
oh, you're
so firm with your thoughts
as though it has
been planned a long time ago

and you had decided to take another path
just like that
baby, just like that
you gave up on our fantasy

just when i thought you're the one
i could trust
i could grow old with
but it was just
a make-believe scene that plays
on my head

you told me you're tired
you needed space
you needed time
for yourself

you decided to leave me
and what am i to you
don't you need me at all, baby

yet, who knows you
better than i do
every move you do
and even the worst in you

after all those years
that we've been together
couldn't you just spare
a word to say if indeed i matter

i thought we are
going to
live up to our
forever years

yet, your mind changed
you could readily
decide to leave our place behind
just like that

i asked that you stay
but oh, you're so firm
with your thoughts
and feelings

and you had decided
to detach from my hands
just like that baby
just like that

* * *

nine

shattered

51

instance

when you left, i thought
my world
shattered
at that instance
i saw you
walking out
through the door and
if only i could put
a stop sign
on your way out
i would do it
even
more than once

if only i could let you realize
perhaps, your mind was somewhat clouded
with worries
or perhaps your view
of our circumstance
was in a blur

you have no clue
how hard and deep this ache could get
as though i could collapse
from where i was
standing

if only i could put myself
out of this misery
my heart would find ease
at this very instance
you and i would be in liberty

* * *

52

predicament

i never thought
i would be in this predicament
what with such long grieving hours

my heart is beating oh-so fast
through the awful graveyard hours

my heart, for sure, needs some kind of nourishing
yet, it keeps calling out for your name

* * *

53

to illuminate

i could cry out
all day and night
still these tears
would keep pouring out

would my heart not
ever get tired
what would it take
so it could then
find its way
to rest

no matter how i try
i would still end up
looking through the sky

then, i would stare at the stars
to illuminate this long, dull, dark night

* * *

54

precious waking hours

countless, sleepless nights
i look through the calendar
to see
what could be
the last
number
or date that i could aim
so that
my helpless wounded heart
could retire

my waking hours
how would i
be able to carry on
what do i do
where do i go
how should i
spend my precious waking hours

* * *

55

wind up

you didn't give me a chance
when i
asked you to stay
you were so
fully decided of leaving
and to be single again

you wanted distance
and space away
from me baby
you found your way
to let me know
there was something
you were looking for

it was very hurting
i don't matter
anymore

more so
i came to hear
you didn't want
to be with me and
spend
another hour
even so
a day or more

leaving was your decision
as you can't take
as you say
being in
the same
direction

but for old time sake
could you say
you've been happy
even once
though i used to believe
it would be lifelong

* * *

56

villain

in your world
i was the villain
the one who caused
your misery and pain

why did i think that
i am the bad
character in
our tale

if we are in some kind of
a superhero story
i wonder who could save
our world
even
for just a day

* * *

57

regain

it wasn't easy yet
i'm working on
accepting
being at peace
within

keep trying to console
my poor soul
yet
my heart would not
listen

trying to regain
my old self
trying to keep
my sanity and
tap into my life's vitality
would my heart's healing time be
of the essence
what would, indeed, help
regain my strength
and confidence

*　*　*

ten

wound and pinch

58

must i

must i console and tell myself
"*Beauty*, you will be all right."

but how could i
when everywhere i look
it's you that i
still would want to see and hold

must i forget about you
must i convince myself
"*Beauty,* you can manage. *You* are smart."

but how could i
when every bit of my thoughts
every beat of my aching heart
each expression i have got
goes out
to you
and only for you

* * *

59

brokenness

have i overlooked myself
what is it that i should do
how do i heal this brokenness
where do i start

how do i say
"*Beauty*, be strong
you will be able to move on
take your time for now
conquer your sorrow
for you will feel better
tomorrow."

* * *

60

face the night

if only
i could face the night
as though nothing at all
has happened
between us

that would be like bringing the old
life back
then how wonderful
would that be
it would be easy
to call it a night

* * *

61

gone wrong

call it shallow
we have our share of
conversations

have i missed out on
your words
or perhaps, on your
expressions

i did not see this coming
i did not anticipate such actions
where have i
gone wrong

* * *

62

gloomy in the mirror

i look through the mirror
and i see
gloomy *Beauty*
lifeless, without care

i couldn't count anymore
the number of days
that had passed
since the last time
i glanced through your weary eyes
because from the time on
every single day
would seem
just the same

again, i looked through the mirror
and i see
restless *Beauty*
helpless, could not start her day

she lost her radiance and tranquility
as though her shining moment had stopped
and still
in disbelief, she could not get up

* * *

63

her own nightmare

she no longer lives up
to her charm
the once confident, loving human
turned into a beast
if not, so dull, almost colourless

she lost her wit
and could not dare
she has now become
Beauty's very own nightmare

* * *

64

interior

into the dining room
i took my steps
i turned the music on
but i could not listen
intently or in passing
every lyric, every sound, and melody
would only remind me
of every part of you and me

i gazed into the left corner
of the living space
it was not so hideous, nor was it flawless

every piece of furniture that sits
on the interior
you bet there was a bit
of dust
but hardly i could look

* * *

65

silver-tinted frame

the silver-tinted little frame
that displays on the corner table
it holds a landscape image
with it comes a sweet message
that reads
"Long live,
Beauty and Tiger!"

that was a small keepsake
we took home
from the souvenir shop one summer
when we visited
our favourite lovely lake

* * *

66

pinch

oh dear, you are very much here
your voice that often tells me
"*Beauty, I* will always be here."
it echoes repetitively

but then, some realization
kicks in
you will not be here again
how could i not
bring that to mind
my *Tiger* is gone

i pinched my left cheek, then the other
oh my gosh
gone, gone
my *Tiger* is
gone in a flash

* * *

67

enough

i'm letting you go
if that's what you want
what's the use of
clinging onto you when
in the end
you said
you would be leaving
just the same

enough for the pain
and all the resentments
the truth remains
it isn't working

it would all be gone
no more worries
when i wake up
it would be a new day
and i should be glad
you'd be out of my sight

go on and find yourself
take your meds or what have you
take care of yourself
we have said enough

* * *

68

numbness

just seven days had past
since you left
i received a text message
saying
hi and how am i
doing

what do i say to that
be friendly and text back
saying, yes i'm okay
and pretend as if
nothing
has happened

the truth is
i have nothing to say
i don't even know
what is this that i feel

emptiness
numbness
i don't even know
if i am making sense

* * *

69

can't help

in such a case, you might want
to see me or to come back
i would not know how my
wounded heart
will react

i don't think at this point
your presence can
help
to ease up
my pain

i don't even know
how should i feel about you
i don't know
if my heart won't ever
be offended again

if being away didn't help
rebuild the relationship
how much else could i trust
that my heart won't ever
get hurt again

* * *

70

maybe then

could we wait
for some time
let this anger be gone
in case that would ever come
maybe then
the light will shine

perhaps--
after the pouring rain has stopped
the sea tide has gone low
the new dawn comes

maybe then
i, *Beauty*
could witness
a new glory
as the sun would shine again
in its brightest

* * *

71

cool and meditative

we could use some
quiet moment
when we do not even have to think
about anything

just be in the moment
empty the space
in our mind
just meditate and cool down

we could call on
positivity
to come
into our life

we could open the door
once more
open our senses
to the sound
of calming
meditative
lyricless music
as both our hearts
could gradually relax

* * *

eleven

∾

seesaw and crack

72

storm

just like how strong
the wind could blow
how lightning could
strike on
a stormy night
that could shock and
make you alert
our romantic world that
we thought
could be as solid as a rock
could vanish any moment

* * *

73

what if

what could we do
if our world must end

or--
what if
our scenario is different

what if
our world could still go on

what if
our days and hours could still go on
what could we say to that

that might sound crazy
even helpless
i know you would tell me
just the same
our world must go on
without each other, and in
a different direction

must i listen to what i hear
must i open my senses
to those words that you whisper
i will try if i could
even if it means
losing you forever

* * *

74

shield

in an instant, you were gone
was that not apparent

it may not be what i wanted or
what i would have wished to happen

nevertheless
i must bring myself
into--
such a huge awakening

let me just tell you this
no matter how strong my shield
could be
i'm just as vulnerable
as any human being could be

* * *

75

very sharp

a part of me has been dislocated like
a bone in an arm that was dislodged
a body in which its core was wrecked
of which i would rather not see or take notice
yet where do i find myself

oh my dear *Tiger*
why did your heart
have to
seek out
change
and that could hurt me
so badly
like there's that object
very sharp
that could strike my deepest
deepest self

* * *

76

random

how could i tell
how my days
would go on

you wanted space
you said this is over
it hurts

it feels as though
you can't see me
you can't hear me

but i'll be okay
like you

i hope soon
i'll be over you
if only
how easy it could be
i'd want to be over you
i know
my feelings will soon be over you
and i will be okay
i'll find my way

***

77

be over

i know this is what you want for me
to be over this misery
don't worry, my *Tiger*
me too
i know
i must overcome such lunacy

i must forbid myself from
having fancy thoughts
because i only continue to bruise
my dear
why must i subject myself to
such discomfort and soreness
if i only knew, my entire being
would end up as though someone
had crushed a car or building
one could bet every piece of me
would be in such a ruin
would i ever want it
would i be out of it

not to disappoint you
i wanted to get over such
feelings and insanity
with the distance
and space that you wanted
i hope you'll find
indeed
what will make you
feel alive again
as will i

* * *

78

better version

shall i keep my head above water
resist the urge
to bring back the shadow of the past
how shall i think of the means to bridge-over
the steps
the hours, the days

i wish to give you
what you wanted for so long
freedom
and happiness
that you said you never
felt
with me ever since

i'm not mad
i'm simply coping
at the end of the day
i know we could be
a better version
of ourselves

it's just a matter of time
and this will soon, perhaps, be consigned
to oblivion
although i could say, i am still in
doubt

* * *

79

new perspective

i pin my hope
and wish that you are just as fine
as new mist, new joys could sprout
in the middle
of a filmy weather
however, that can be predictable

being away with distance and time
focusing on a move that highlights
glitter even through the very edge of a corner
can help mend
the almost impossible thing to occur
my deeply wounded heart can soon
find its way to the easing point

what could be a better idea
than learning to express
oneself
and learning what it means
to take a glimpse, grinning from ear to ear
even for just a minute or some seconds

even though we both have
tried to master strokes
take a shot amid ambivalence
there's that aspect within us
that can point us to a new
perspective

and that we could be
better off
taking a different route
we do not have
to be loud

* * *

80

awesome people

could we just remain
genial
if not, link two familiar people
who could be benevolent
to each other
though on a different
level
just like what you suggest
and i could try to
believe
in that promise as well

and even if it may lacerate
just to forgo the thought
the fanciful merriment of romance
remoteness from our outside world
that ended in an entanglement
what matters
in the end, is
if we could be in tune
or at peace

and i call on
the *Supreme Power*
that we could move on
see through a restful second
free from disturbance
even if it may seem soundless
we could hear and sense things
through a different
yet better horizon

let's not lose
the bond that
we've built
we're awesome people
after all
and we've known
each other that long
and oh so well

* * *

twelve

sundown to sunup

81

new glow

after the rain, the exterior dries up again
it is a welcoming occurrence
it is nature's way of manifesting life

we could point to why we exist
or we could just be in it

you could point to yours
i could zero in on mine
make it bear fruits and limes

in some way
we could deconstruct or assemble
bits and pieces of our life
solve a puzzle
get out of a mess

but --
how do we get out
and clear out
our thoughts
yet be inspired from the past

in whatever track
we decide to take
life is sublime not to immerse
through its wonders

acknowledge
a new creation
see beauty from
a new angle

the new horizon unfolds
as you wake up to the sunrise with
a mesmerizing glow

* * *

82

to feel again

there's some thrill in seeking, seeing
a new compass
find such an unexplored part of myself
flip over when i follow through a new scent
it can be superficial
or it could grow deep, who knows

a new world of love could be as pretty as a picture
setting a new mood, feel a raw texture
or it could be peculiar, or whatever it could be
and even if it may not be with you
that would be fine, though
i could not be sure
that can remain
to be seen

i long for some delights and treats
that can trigger
the glimmer in my eyes
to witness an energized, emboldened look
as i face
the no longer dusty, bewildered
reflection
as i stand up to see *Beauty* in her
two point-O attempt

it gives me pleasure
to come to my senses and be in touch
with who i am and what i can be
aren't i a charmer
with whom someone can fancy
and meet me half-way

i yearn to sprinkle with my loving spirit
to be in someone's arms
it would be good to try
to lay entwined with arms wrapped around

oh, i love the feeling
the warmth, the touch
it makes me feel alive
fresh and enriching
to feel good again and
face new challenges
i should be ready for it and
say, it can be wonderful
be in an exciting world of
new love's miracle

* * *

83

just wish

do not dwell on a thought
i may go through sporadic restlessness
even i may have a jittery, twitchy sleep
and wake up to a beeping sound

if you ask
i just wish for your
happiness
that you may find what
you are
indeed looking for

be happy baby
be happy
even if
i'm not the one
you're looking for

i cherish the happy times
the fun ones
and even those that were not so fine

life goes on
from here on
and i wish
you will find your happiness

* * *

84

part

hurrah for all
you've done
and i'm grateful
for all
those things

look after yourself and
you will
always remain
part of
my whole being

it doesn't matter
if you are someone
from my past
i won't ever get to today
nor my future
if i won't ever learn to look back

after all, you are
someone with whom my world
i used to share
goodbye, my old pal *Tiger*

* * *

85

indescribably wonderful

i can't wait for my climactic moment
it can stir, it can be riveting
seeing and enjoying
a life of being
by my strong self again
like any happy
single human

i look forward to a chance to experience
self-love, it doesn't matter
if i am unattached, unconnected
i long to see life in
a different view
even if i can be like a spectator

i look forward
to be victorious over my fear
to get to know inward
myself again
to become closer
to my *Creator*

i look forward
to be with my family
to discover
new space, expand if need be
to discover whatever else
God wants me to try like a co-creator

i look forward
to become stronger
like a fortress-like structure
that seems indestructible
to paint the unfamiliar canvas
to master some lyrics and hymns
to meet a few new people
to take another round

i look forward
to pursue new passions
to navigate what my new world can offer
to travel, to go cross-country, and more
to see adorable places
to seek some more adventures

life, after all, is good
i can't wait to tap
into my newly found energy
i welcome life
i say hello
to the new
faces i meet
my indescribably wonderful future
awaits

* * *

other books by the author

Other Fiction and Poetry Books

Feed and Discern:
Some Words of Wisdom, Some Poems, Some Life Lessons

Tweets for Your Thoughts

A Wacky, Rocky World: Just a Teeny Little Voice

about the author

Sheila Atienza is a Canadian book author, digital media artist, and marketing professional based in B.C., Canada. She is also an award-winning filmmaker, actress, and passionate content creator.

Sheila explores nonfiction, fiction, and poetry. Some of her published works/books are available in:

University of Toronto Thomas Fisher Library; McGill University; Dalhousie University DAL Killam Library; Brown University; Library and Archives nationales du Québec; Canada Mortgage Housing Corporation; Medicine Hat College; Loyalist College; and other libraries across Canada and the U.S.A.

Sheila's books are also available through bookstores and online retailers worldwide.

www.ingramcontent.com/pod-product-compliance
Lightning Source LLC
Chambersburg PA
CBHW021425070526
44577CB00001B/56